Ssssh!

C000003098

Don't tell everyone, bu

WE'RE

*Come and find a treasure that keeps getting MORE,
the MORE you spend! Unscramble the letters:*

R   Y   P   R

E   A

1

Sssssh!

Put a timer on for one minute

Sit together and LISTEN until the timer goes off

What is prayer anyway?

What did you hear?

Why do you think we pray?

How easy was it?

How easy is it to talk to God?

How easy is it to listen to God?

Let's go look round the Treasury!

Where shall we explore first?

Welcome to the Great Hall

This is where we spend most of our time doing ordinary, everyday things. Where is that for you? We can pray here every day too.

Match up the beginnings and the endings:

Saying thank you to the **Lord Jesus** for meals...

Asking the **Lord** to bless us as we leave home...

Telling the **Lord God** about our day at bedtime...

... gives us purple spots.

... reminds us **God**'s with us everywhere we go.

... reminds us where our food comes from.

... gives us hiccups.

... makes us feel safe and loved.

... makes cucumbers grow from our noses.

... reminds us to brush our teeth.

5

Welcome to the Ancient Crypt

People have been praying for many, many years. They've left us a storehouse full of treasure.

How does this make you feel?
Circle the emojis or draw your own.

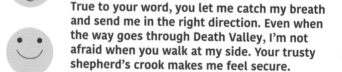 **Psalm 23** (The Message version)

God, my shepherd! I don't need a thing. You have bedded me down in lush meadows, you find me quiet pools to drink from.

True to your word, you let me catch my breath and send me in the right direction. Even when the way goes through Death Valley, I'm not afraid when you walk at my side. Your trusty shepherd's crook makes me feel secure.

You serve me a six-course dinner right in front of my enemies. You revive my drooping head; my cup brims with blessing. Your beauty and love chase after me every day of my life. I'm back home in the house of God for the rest of my life.

Prayers to learn

The Lord bless you and keep you.
The Lord make his face shine on
you and be gracious to you.
The Lord turn his face towards
you and give you peace.
(Moses in Numbers 6)

Alone with none but you, O God,
I journey on my way.
What need I fear
when you are near,
O King of night and day?
More safe am I within your hands
than if an army round me stands.
(St Columba)

And there are so many more!

To learn a prayer, you can...

*Throw a ball to
someone who says
the next
line...*

*Make up
actions to
go with the
words...*

*Find a tune to sing
the words to...*

*Say one word each
round the table...*

2
Your kingdom come, your will be done on earth as in heaven.

2
Sad people

1
People on the edge

T[he]
Lor[d's]
Pray[er]
is t[he]
pray[er]

1
Our Father in heaven, hallowed be your name.

3
Give us today our daily bread.

3
God's people

Roll a dice twice to see which part of the prayer to pray and who to pray for today. Talk and pray about them.

8

4
Forgive us our sins as we forgive those who sin against us.

4
People who care

5
Lead us not into temptation but deliver us from evil.

5
Happy people

6
For the kingdom, the power and the glory are yours, now and forever. Amen

6
Hurting people

at
sus
ught
s best
iends

Other ancient ways to pray use objects like beads, a cross, a candle, a picture or incense.

Sometimes a 'thing' helps us concentrate.

Leave one person on a chair. Everyone else go and look for an object to hold while you pray. Come back together and talk about why you chose it from all the things in your house.

Pirates go in search of treasure. One last ancient prayer is by a sailor – Sir Francis Drake (some people called him a pirate!):

Colour the ship

Disturb us, Lord, when we are too well pleased with ourselves, when our dreams have come true because we have dreamed too little, when we arrived safely because we sailed too close to the shore.

Disturb us, Lord, when with the abundance of things we possess, we have lost our thirst for the waters of life; having fallen in love with life, we have ceased to dream of eternity and in our efforts to build a new earth, we have allowed our vision of the new heaven to dim.

Doodle a border

Welcome to the Inventors' Workshop

If God had a phone...

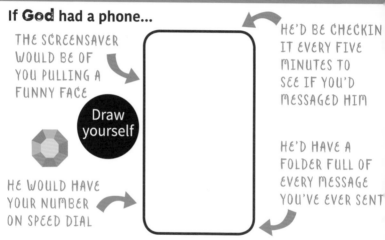

THE SCREENSAVER WOULD BE OF YOU PULLING A FUNNY FACE

Draw yourself

HE'D BE CHECKIN IT EVERY FIVE MINUTES TO SEE IF YOU'D MESSAGED HIM

HE WOULD HAVE YOUR NUMBER ON SPEED DIAL

HE'D HAVE A FOLDER FULL OF EVERY MESSAGE YOU'VE EVER SENT

You are unique to God!

Only you can know him like you know him!

So you might need new ways to pray as well as old ones.

ings we see outside and inside can remind us of how
onderful God is. He's safer than a house, stronger than a
lldozer. Everything we see can remind us to talk to him!

utside, **God**, you are....

And inside?

And inside, **God**, you are...

Invent-a-prayer

My friend Loving Spirit
Jesus
Lord Dear Father

1 Tell God who you think he is

You are amazing
I know you love
You turned water into wine

2 Tell him what you think he's like

We're really glad
We're a bit sad today

3 Tell him how you are

We're worried about Syria
Please look after Grand

4 Tell him what you need

5 Say why you trust him to listen to you

In the name of the Father, Son and Holy Spirit

In Jesus' name

Bye
I love you
Amen Thank you

6 Sign off

Welcome to the Alchemists' Den

Where rubbish changes into pure gold

What rubbish in the world needs changing?
Draw it in the bubbles. Ask God to transform them.

We can't always spot the difference prayer makes.

Can you find all 15 differences?

But we know it does make a difference.

17

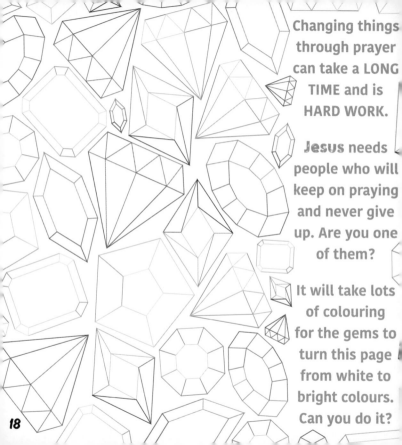

Changing things through prayer can take a LONG TIME and is HARD WORK.

Jesus needs people who will keep on praying and never give up. Are you one of them?

It will take lots of colouring for the gems to turn this page from white to bright colours. Can you do it?

18

Five 'fings' on five fingers
(Or four fingers and a 'fumb')

Here's a hand for everyone in your family and maybe a friend or two. Write a name of someone to pray for on each finger. Then pray for them on your real fingers.

When we go through rubbish times, God can change them to treasure through the wonder of prayer. Here are a few Bible prayers you can use too.

There is no one holy like the Lord; there is no one besides you; there is no Rock like our God.
Hannah (1 Samuel 2)

I keep asking that the God of our Lord Jesus Christ, the glorious Father, may give you the Spirit of wisdom and revelation, so that you may know him better.
Paul praying for his friends (Ephesians 1)

Why, my soul, are you downcast? Why so disturbed within me? Put your hope in God, for I will yet praise him, my Saviour and my God.
Psalm 42

Father, I thank you that you have heard me. I knew that you always hear me.
Jesus (John 11)

Sovereign Lord, remember me. Please, God, strengthen me just once more.
Samson (Judges 16)

Jesus, remember me when you come into your kingdom.
The thief on the cross (Luke 23)

God, have mercy on me, a sinner.
The tax collector in Jesus' parable (Luke 18)

Which do you like best? Can you memorise it? (see p. 7)

20

Welcome to the Shower Room

WHAT A MESS I'VE MADE OF THINGS! POOH! YUK!

Gallons of grace

JUST WHAT I NEED!

Gallons of grace

BUT HOW DOES IT START?

Gallons of grace

Try a sorry prayer!

What could they say?

Gallons of grace

Welcome to the Chamber of Mystery

Some people think prayer is like a vending machine

PRAYER IN

NICE THINGS OUT

Or an arcade game

PRAYER IN

SOMETIMES YOU WIN
SOMETIMES YOU LOSE

Or a cash machine

PRAYER IN

WHAT YOU ARE OWED

22

But the Lord God is God

Light three candles.

Sit and watch them quietly.

 Think about God the Father,
God the Son,
God the Holy Spirit.

God's ways are higher than our ways
and his thoughts are higher than our thoughts.

Jesus-people call this 'mystery'.

It's not comfortable. We don't enjoy it. We can't explain it

We see through a glass darkly

Poetry   Art

The dark night of the soul

A cloud of unknowing

I wonder   No sense   Aw

A fiery, cloudy pillar   How long, O God?

Where are you, God?

Questions   It's not fai

Welcome to the Rocket Launchpad

Sometimes we shoot up prayers like ROCKETS.
Anytime. Anywhere. Maybe one word!

Where's the prayer these angels have spotted?
Draw an X in the right square.

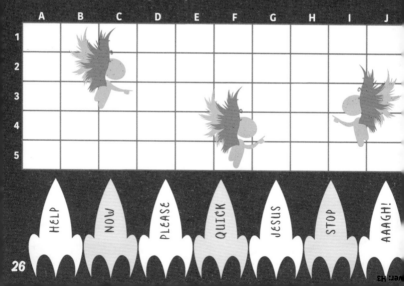

PRIVATE QUARTERS

NO ENTRY

Except the

••

family

(Fill in your family name)

Our special prayers

At mealtimes

At bedtime

When we go away from each other

The people we pray for

Store up for yourselves treasures in heaven... for where your treasure is, there your heart will be also.
Jesus (Matthew 6:20–21)

How full is your treasury in heaven?

emember the great thing about the treasure of prayer? ook back at page 1.) How about going back through his book and doing it all again?

S. Seek and you will find: *did you find a jewel on each page?*

The Bible Reading Fellowship
15 The Chambers, Vineyard
Abingdon OX14 3FE
brf.org.uk

The Bible Reading Fellowship (BRF) is a Registered Charity (233280)

ISBN 978 0 85746 715 7
First published 2018
10 9 8 7 6 5 4 3 2 1 0
All rights reserved

Text by Lucy Moore 2018
This edition © The Bible Reading Fellowship 2018
Illustrations by Rebecca J Hall

The author asserts the moral right to be identified as the author of this work

Acknowledgements
Unless otherwise stated, scripture quotations taken from The Holy Bible, New
International Version (Anglicised edition) copyright © 1979, 1984, 2011 by Biblica. Used
by permission of Hodder & Stoughton Publishers, a Hachette UK company. All rights
reserved. 'NIV' is a registered trademark of Biblica. UK trademark number 1448790.

Scripture quotations are taken from The Message, copyright © 1993, 1994, 1995, 1996,
2000, 2001, 2002 by Eugene H. Peterson. Used by permission of NavPress. All rights
reserved. Represented by Tyndale House Publishers, Inc.

A catalogue record for this book is available from the British Library

Printed and bound in the UK by Zenith Media NP4 0DQ